Welcome to The

Ultimate Boss

PLANNER

One of the vital techniques to becoming a successful entrepreneur is setting goals and creating a plan to implement them. Another important technique of successful bosses is being organized and staying organized. An empire cannot be built in chaos, so use this Ultimate Boss Planner to help you set goals and become organized.

Dr. Synovia Dover-Harris
CEO of A2Z Books Publishing

"

Failing to Plan is Planning to Fail

Benjamin Franklin

This Planner Belongs to:

_____

_____

_____

What are your *Entrepreneurial goals?*

GOAL /gōl/
Is defined as the object of a person's ambition or effort; an aim or desired result.

_____

_____

_____

Are your goals *Smart Goals?*

Smart means:

Specific

(Is it clearly defined?)

_____

_____

Measureable

(How can you measure this?)

_____

_____

Achievable

(Can you actually achieve this?)

_____

_____

Relevant

(Does it make sense to do?)

_____

_____

Timely

(When does it need to be completed by?)

_____

_____

_____

You should get goals beyond

Your Reach

so you always have

Something To Live For

TED TURNER

What steps do I need to take to reach my goals?

_____

_____

_____

_____

_____

_____

How much time will it take?

_____

_____

_____

_____

_____

_____

How much money will it take?

_____

_____

_____

_____

_____

_____

What steps do I need to take to reach my goals?

_____

_____

_____

_____

_____

_____

How much time will it take?

_____

_____

_____

_____

_____

How much money will it take?

_____

_____

_____

_____

_____

My ultimate goal
is to be

Better Today

Than
YESTERDAY

What are your accountability measures? (How will you measure the achievement of your goals)?

_____

_____

_____

_____

_____

_____

What is your motivation?

_____

_____

_____

_____

_____

_____

NOTE:

In order to achieve your long-term goals you must cut them down into short-term goals that will help you accomplish the small steps you need to take in order to accomplish your long-term goals.

For example:

If your main goal is to start a hair business, your short-term goals to accomplish this long-term goal are things like:

- Obtaining a website
- Obtaining a logo
- Obtaining your LLC
- Finding a Hair Vendor
- Determining where you will run your business
- Etc.

Month: _____

SUNDAY	MONDAY	TUESDAY	WEDNESDAY

THURSDAY	FRIDAY	SATURDAY

Notes

_____
_____
_____
_____
_____
_____
_____
_____
_____
_____
_____
_____
_____
_____
_____
_____
_____
_____
_____
_____
_____
_____
_____
_____

THIS WEEK *Goals*

MONDAY _____

_____

_____

TUESDAY _____

_____

_____

WEDNESDAY _____

_____

_____

THURSDAY _____

_____

_____

FRIDAY _____

_____

_____

SATURDAY _____

_____

_____

SUNDAY _____

_____

_____

THIS WEEK *Schedule*

MONDAY
AM	PM	AM	PM

TUESDAY
AM	PM	AM	PM

WEDNESDAY
AM	PM	AM	PM

THURSDAY
AM	PM	AM	PM

FRIDAY
AM	PM	AM	PM

SATURDAY
AM	PM	AM	PM

SUNDAY
AM	PM	AM	PM

THIS WEEK *Goals*

MONDAY _____
_____
_____

TUESDAY _____
_____
_____

WEDNESDAY _____
_____
_____

THURSDAY _____
_____
_____

FRIDAY _____
_____
_____

SATURDAY _____
_____
_____

SUNDAY _____
_____
_____

THIS WEEK *Schedule*

MONDAY

AM	PM	AM	PM

TUESDAY

AM	PM	AM	PM

WEDNESDAY

AM	PM	AM	PM

THURSDAY

AM	PM	AM	PM

FRIDAY

AM	PM	AM	PM

SATURDAY

AM	PM	AM	PM

SUNDAY

AM	PM	AM	PM

MID MONTH *Checklist*

Am I on track to accomplish my goals?

_____
_____
_____
_____
_____
_____

What are my accountability measures?

_____
_____
_____
_____
_____
_____

What have I accomplished so far?

_____
_____
_____
_____
_____
_____

On a scale from 1 to 10 how close am I to reaching my goals

○ ○ ○ ○ ○ ○ ○ ○ ○ ○
1 2 3 4 5 6 7 8 9 10

Notes

THIS WEEK *Goals*

MONDAY _____
_____
_____

TUESDAY _____
_____
_____

WEDNESDAY _____
_____
_____

THURSDAY _____
_____
_____

FRIDAY _____
_____
_____

SATURDAY _____
_____
_____

SUNDAY _____
_____
_____

THIS WEEK *Schedule*

MONDAY
AM	PM	AM	PM

TUESDAY
AM	PM	AM	PM

WEDNESDAY
AM	PM	AM	PM

THURSDAY
AM	PM	AM	PM

FRIDAY
AM	PM	AM	PM

SATURDAY
AM	PM	AM	PM

SUNDAY
AM	PM	AM	PM

THIS WEEK *Goals*

MONDAY _____
_____
_____

TUESDAY _____
_____
_____

WEDNESDAY _____
_____
_____

THURSDAY _____
_____
_____

FRIDAY _____
_____
_____

SATURDAY _____
_____
_____

SUNDAY _____
_____
_____

THIS WEEK *Schedule*

MONDAY
AM	PM	AM	PM

TUESDAY
AM	PM	AM	PM

WEDNESDAY
AM	PM	AM	PM

THURSDAY
AM	PM	AM	PM

FRIDAY
AM	PM	AM	PM

SATURDAY
AM	PM	AM	PM

SUNDAY
AM	PM	AM	PM

What did I accomplish this month?

_____
_____
_____
_____

Did I meet my goals?

_____
_____
_____
_____

If not, what do I need to do to differently to accomplish my goals?

_____
_____
_____
_____

A goal without a plan is
Just a Wish

THINK *Tank*

Think Tank n/-
A place where ideas are formed
Use this page to write about new ideas and things you are thinking about.

_____
_____
_____
_____
_____
_____
_____
_____
_____
_____
_____
_____
_____
_____
_____
_____
_____
_____
_____
_____
_____
_____

Affirmations

/əfərˈmāSH(ə)n/
Words of encouragement and motivation.
Use this page to write motivational content.

Notes

Month: _____

SUNDAY	MONDAY	TUESDAY	WEDNESDAY

THURSDAY	FRIDAY	SATURDAY

Notes

_____
_____
_____
_____
_____
_____
_____
_____
_____
_____
_____
_____
_____
_____
_____
_____
_____
_____
_____
_____
_____
_____
_____
_____
_____
_____
_____

THIS WEEK *Goals*

MONDAY _____
_____
_____

TUESDAY _____
_____
_____

WEDNESDAY _____
_____
_____

THURSDAY _____
_____
_____

FRIDAY _____
_____
_____

SATURDAY _____
_____
_____

SUNDAY _____
_____
_____

THIS WEEK *Schedule*

MONDAY

AM	PM	AM	PM

TUESDAY

AM	PM	AM	PM

WEDNESDAY

AM	PM	AM	PM

THURSDAY

AM	PM	AM	PM

FRIDAY

AM	PM	AM	PM

SATURDAY

AM	PM	AM	PM

SUNDAY

AM	PM	AM	PM

THIS WEEK *Goals*

MONDAY _____
_____
_____

TUESDAY _____
_____
_____

WEDNESDAY _____
_____
_____

THURSDAY _____
_____
_____

FRIDAY _____
_____
_____

SATURDAY _____
_____
_____

SUNDAY _____
_____
_____

THIS WEEK *Schedule*

MONDAY

AM	PM	AM	PM

TUESDAY

AM	PM	AM	PM

WEDNESDAY

AM	PM	AM	PM

THURSDAY

AM	PM	AM	PM

FRIDAY

AM	PM	AM	PM

SATURDAY

AM	PM	AM	PM

SUNDAY

AM	PM	AM	PM

MID MONTH *Checklist*

Am I on track to accomplish my goals?

_____
_____
_____
_____
_____
_____

What are my accountability measures?

_____
_____
_____
_____
_____
_____

What have I accomplished so far?

_____
_____
_____
_____
_____
_____

On a scale from 1 to 10 how close am I toreaching my goals

○ ○ ○ ○ ○ ○ ○ ○ ○ ○
1   2   3   4   5   6   7   8   9 10

Notes

THIS WEEK *Goals*

MONDAY _____
_____
_____

TUESDAY _____
_____
_____

WEDNESDAY _____
_____
_____

THURSDAY _____
_____
_____

FRIDAY _____
_____
_____

SATURDAY _____
_____
_____

SUNDAY _____
_____
_____

THIS WEEK *Schedule*

MONDAY
AM	PM	AM	PM

TUESDAY
AM	PM	AM	PM

WEDNESDAY
AM	PM	AM	PM

THURSDAY
AM	PM	AM	PM

FRIDAY
AM	PM	AM	PM

SATURDAY
AM	PM	AM	PM

SUNDAY
AM	PM	AM	PM

THIS WEEK *Goals*

MONDAY _____
_____
_____

TUESDAY _____
_____
_____

WEDNESDAY _____
_____
_____

THURSDAY _____
_____
_____

FRIDAY _____
_____
_____

SATURDAY _____
_____
_____

SUNDAY _____
_____
_____

THIS WEEK *Schedule*

MONDAY
AM	PM	AM	PM

TUESDAY
AM	PM	AM	PM

WEDNESDAY
AM	PM	AM	PM

THURSDAY
AM	PM	AM	PM

FRIDAY
AM	PM	AM	PM

SATURDAY
AM	PM	AM	PM

SUNDAY
AM	PM	AM	PM

MONTHLY *Closeout*

What did I accomplish this month?

_____

_____

_____

_____

Did I meet my goals?

_____

_____

_____

_____

If not, what do I need to do to differently to accomplish my goals?

_____

_____

_____

_____

A goal without a plan is
Just a Wish

THINK *Tank*

Think Tank n/-
A place where ideas are formed
Use this page to write about new ideas and things you are thinking about.

_____

_____

_____

_____

_____

_____

_____

_____

_____

_____

_____

_____

_____

_____

_____

_____

_____

_____

_____

_____

_____

_____

Affirmations

/afərˈmāSH(ə)n/
Words of encouragement and motivation.
Use this page to write motivational content.

Always deliver
more than
What is expected !

Month: _____

SUNDAY	MONDAY	TUESDAY	WEDNESDAY

THURSDAY	FRIDAY	SATURDAY	Notes

THIS WEEK *Goals*

MONDAY _____
_____
_____

TUESDAY _____
_____
_____

WEDNESDAY _____
_____
_____

THURSDAY _____
_____
_____

FRIDAY _____
_____
_____

SATURDAY _____
_____
_____

SUNDAY _____
_____
_____

THIS WEEK *Schedule*

MONDAY
AM	PM	AM	PM

TUESDAY
AM	PM	AM	PM

WEDNESDAY
AM	PM	AM	PM

THURSDAY
AM	PM	AM	PM

FRIDAY
AM	PM	AM	PM

SATURDAY
AM	PM	AM	PM

SUNDAY
AM	PM	AM	PM

THIS WEEK *Goals*

MONDAY _____
_____
_____

TUESDAY _____
_____
_____

WEDNESDAY _____
_____
_____

THURSDAY _____
_____
_____

FRIDAY _____
_____
_____

SATURDAY _____
_____
_____

SUNDAY _____
_____
_____

THIS WEEK *Schedule*

MONDAY
AM	PM	AM	PM

TUESDAY
AM	PM	AM	PM

WEDNESDAY
AM	PM	AM	PM

THURSDAY
AM	PM	AM	PM

FRIDAY
AM	PM	AM	PM

SATURDAY
AM	PM	AM	PM

SUNDAY
AM	PM	AM	PM

MID MONTH *Checklist*

Am I on track to accomplish my goals?

_____
_____
_____
_____
_____
_____

What are my accountability measures?

_____
_____
_____
_____
_____
_____

What have I accomplished so far?

_____
_____
_____
_____
_____

On a scale from 1 to 10 how close am I toreaching my goals

○ ○ ○ ○ ○ ○ ○ ○ ○ ○
1   2   3   4   5   6   7   8   9   10

Notes

THIS WEEK *Goals*

MONDAY _____
_____
_____

TUESDAY _____
_____
_____

WEDNESDAY _____
_____
_____

THURSDAY _____
_____
_____

FRIDAY _____
_____
_____

SATURDAY _____
_____
_____

SUNDAY _____
_____
_____

THIS WEEK *Schedule*

MONDAY

AM	PM	AM	PM

TUESDAY

AM	PM	AM	PM

WEDNESDAY

AM	PM	AM	PM

THURSDAY

AM	PM	AM	PM

FRIDAY

AM	PM	AM	PM

SATURDAY

AM	PM	AM	PM

SUNDAY

AM	PM	AM	PM

THIS WEEK *Goals*

MONDAY _____
_____
_____

TUESDAY _____
_____
_____

WEDNESDAY _____
_____
_____

THURSDAY _____
_____
_____

FRIDAY _____
_____
_____

SATURDAY _____
_____
_____

SUNDAY _____
_____
_____

THIS WEEK *Schedule*

MONDAY

AM | PM | AM | PM

TUESDAY

AM | PM | AM | PM

WEDNESDAY

AM | PM | AM | PM

THURSDAY

AM | PM | AM | PM

FRIDAY

AM | PM | AM | PM

SATURDAY

AM | PM | AM | PM

SUNDAY

AM | PM | AM | PM

What did I accomplish this month?

_____

_____

_____

_____

Did I meet my goals?

_____

_____

_____

_____

If not, what do I need to do to differently to accomplish my goals?

_____

_____

_____

_____

A goal without a plan is
Just a Wish

THINK *Tank*

Think Tank n/-
A place where ideas are formed
Use this page to write about new ideas and things you are thinking about.

_____
_____
_____
_____
_____
_____
_____
_____
_____
_____
_____
_____
_____
_____
_____
_____
_____
_____
_____
_____
_____
_____
_____
_____
_____

Affirmations

/afərˈmāSH(ə)n/
Words of encouragement and motivation.
Use this page to write motivational content.

_____
_____
_____
_____
_____
_____
_____
_____
_____
_____
_____
_____
_____
_____
_____
_____
_____
_____
_____
_____
_____
_____

Notes

Month: _____

SUNDAY	MONDAY	TUESDAY	WEDNESDAY

THURSDAY	FRIDAY	SATURDAY	Notes

THIS WEEK *Goals*

MONDAY _____
_____
_____

TUESDAY _____
_____
_____

WEDNESDAY _____
_____
_____

THURSDAY _____
_____
_____

FRIDAY _____
_____
_____

SATURDAY _____
_____
_____

SUNDAY _____
_____
_____

THIS WEEK *Schedule*

MONDAY

AM	PM	AM	PM

TUESDAY

AM	PM	AM	PM

WEDNESDAY

AM	PM	AM	PM

THURSDAY

AM	PM	AM	PM

FRIDAY

AM	PM	AM	PM

SATURDAY

AM	PM	AM	PM

SUNDAY

AM	PM	AM	PM

THIS WEEK *Goals*

MONDAY _____
_____
_____

TUESDAY _____
_____
_____

WEDNESDAY _____
_____
_____

THURSDAY _____
_____
_____

FRIDAY _____
_____
_____

SATURDAY _____
_____
_____

SUNDAY _____
_____
_____

THIS WEEK *Schedule*

MONDAY

AM	PM	AM	PM

TUESDAY

AM	PM	AM	PM

WEDNESDAY

AM	PM	AM	PM

THURSDAY

AM	PM	AM	PM

FRIDAY

AM	PM	AM	PM

SATURDAY

AM	PM	AM	PM

SUNDAY

AM	PM	AM	PM

MID MONTH *Checklist*

Am I on track to accomplish my goals?

_____
_____
_____
_____
_____
_____

What are my accountability measures?

_____
_____
_____
_____
_____
_____

What have I accomplished so far?

_____
_____
_____
_____
_____
_____

On a scale from 1 to 10 how close am I toreaching my goals

○   ○   ○   ○   ○   ○   ○   ○   ○   ○
1   2   3   4   5   6   7   8   9   10

Notes

THIS WEEK *Goals*

MONDAY _____

_____

_____

TUESDAY _____

_____

_____

WEDNESDAY _____

_____

_____

THURSDAY _____

_____

_____

FRIDAY _____

_____

_____

SATURDAY _____

_____

_____

SUNDAY _____

_____

_____

THIS WEEK *Schedule*

MONDAY _____
AM	PM	AM	PM

TUESDAY _____
AM	PM	AM	PM

WEDNESDAY _____
AM	PM	AM	PM

THURSDAY _____
AM	PM	AM	PM

FRIDAY _____
AM	PM	AM	PM

SATURDAY _____
AM	PM	AM	PM

SUNDAY _____
AM	PM	AM	PM

THIS WEEK *Goals*

MONDAY _____
_____
_____

TUESDAY _____
_____
_____

WEDNESDAY _____
_____
_____

THURSDAY _____
_____
_____

FRIDAY _____
_____
_____

SATURDAY _____
_____
_____

SUNDAY _____
_____
_____

THIS WEEK *Schedule*

MONDAY
AM	PM	AM	PM

TUESDAY
AM	PM	AM	PM

WEDNESDAY
AM	PM	AM	PM

THURSDAY
AM	PM	AM	PM

FRIDAY
AM	PM	AM	PM

SATURDAY
AM	PM	AM	PM

SUNDAY
AM	PM	AM	PM

What did I accomplish this month?

_____

_____

_____

_____

Did I meet my goals?

_____

_____

_____

_____

If not, what do I need to do to differently to accomplish my goals?

_____

_____

_____

_____

A goal without a plan is
Just a Wish

THINK *Tank*

Think Tank n/-
A place where ideas are formed
Use this page to write about new ideas and things you are thinking about.

_____
_____
_____
_____
_____
_____
_____
_____
_____
_____
_____
_____
_____
_____
_____
_____
_____
_____
_____
_____
_____

Affirmations

/əfərˈmāSH(ə)n/

Words of encouragement and motivation.
Use this page to write motivational content.

_____
_____
_____
_____
_____
_____
_____
_____
_____
_____
_____
_____
_____
_____
_____
_____
_____
_____
_____
_____
_____
_____
_____
_____

Quality is the Best
Business Plan

John Lasseter

Month: _____

SUNDAY	MONDAY	TUESDAY	WEDNESDAY

THURSDAY	FRIDAY	SATURDAY	Notes
			_____
			_____
			_____
			_____
			_____
			_____
			_____
			_____
			_____
			_____
			_____
			_____
			_____
			_____
			_____
			_____
			_____
			_____
			_____
			_____
			_____
			_____
			_____
			_____

THIS WEEK *Goals*

MONDAY
_____
_____
_____

TUESDAY
_____
_____
_____

WEDNESDAY
_____
_____
_____

THURSDAY
_____
_____
_____

FRIDAY
_____
_____
_____

SATURDAY
_____
_____
_____

SUNDAY
_____
_____
_____

THIS WEEK *Schedule*

MONDAY
AM	PM	AM	PM

TUESDAY
AM	PM	AM	PM

WEDNESDAY
AM	PM	AM	PM

THURSDAY
AM	PM	AM	PM

FRIDAY
AM	PM	AM	PM

SATURDAY
AM	PM	AM	PM

SUNDAY
AM	PM	AM	PM

THIS WEEK *Goals*

MONDAY _____
_____
_____

TUESDAY _____
_____
_____

WEDNESDAY _____
_____
_____

THURSDAY _____
_____
_____

FRIDAY _____
_____
_____

SATURDAY _____
_____
_____

SUNDAY _____
_____
_____

THIS WEEK *Schedule*

MONDAY _____
AM   PM   AM   PM

TUESDAY _____
AM   PM   AM   PM

WEDNESDAY _____
AM   PM   AM   PM

THURSDAY _____
AM   PM   AM   PM

FRIDAY _____
AM   PM   AM   PM

SATURDAY _____
AM   PM   AM   PM

SUNDAY _____
AM   PM   AM   PM

MID MONTH *Checklist*

Am I on track to accomplish my goals?

_____

_____

_____

_____

_____

_____

What are my accountability measures?

_____

_____

_____

_____

_____

_____

What have I accomplished so far?

_____

_____

_____

_____

_____

_____

On a scale from 1 to 10 how close am I to reaching my goals

○　○　○　○　○　○　○　○　○　○
1　2　3　4　5　6　7　8　9　10

Notes

THIS WEEK *Goals*

MONDAY _____
_____
_____

TUESDAY _____
_____
_____

WEDNESDAY _____
_____
_____

THURSDAY _____
_____
_____

FRIDAY _____
_____
_____

SATURDAY _____
_____
_____

SUNDAY _____
_____
_____

THIS WEEK *Schedule*

MONDAY
AM	PM	AM	PM

TUESDAY
AM	PM	AM	PM

WEDNESDAY
AM	PM	AM	PM

THURSDAY
AM	PM	AM	PM

FRIDAY
AM	PM	AM	PM

SATURDAY
AM	PM	AM	PM

SUNDAY
AM	PM	AM	PM

THIS WEEK *Goals*

MONDAY
_____
_____
_____

TUESDAY
_____
_____
_____

WEDNESDAY
_____
_____
_____

THURSDAY
_____
_____
_____

FRIDAY
_____
_____
_____

SATURDAY
_____
_____
_____

SUNDAY
_____
_____
_____

THIS WEEK *Schedule*

MONDAY

AM	PM	AM	PM

TUESDAY

AM	PM	AM	PM

WEDNESDAY

AM	PM	AM	PM

THURSDAY

AM	PM	AM	PM

FRIDAY

AM	PM	AM	PM

SATURDAY

AM	PM	AM	PM

SUNDAY

AM	PM	AM	PM

What did I accomplish this month?

_____

_____

_____

_____

Did I meet my goals?

_____

_____

_____

_____

If not, what do I need to do to differently to accomplish my goals?

_____

_____

_____

_____

A goal without a plan is
Just a Wish

THINK *Tank*

Think Tank n/-
A place where ideas are formed
Use this page to write about new ideas and things you are thinking about.

_____
_____
_____
_____
_____
_____
_____
_____
_____
_____
_____
_____
_____
_____
_____
_____
_____
_____
_____
_____
_____
_____
_____

Affirmations

/əfərˈmāSH(ə)n/

Words of encouragement and motivation.
Use this page to write motivational content.

_____
_____
_____
_____
_____
_____
_____
_____
_____
_____
_____
_____
_____
_____
_____
_____
_____
_____
_____
_____
_____
_____
_____
_____
_____
_____

Notes

Month: _____

SUNDAY	MONDAY	TUESDAY	WEDNESDAY

THURSDAY	FRIDAY	SATURDAY

THIS WEEK *Goals*

MONDAY
_____
_____
_____

TUESDAY
_____
_____
_____

WEDNESDAY
_____
_____
_____

THURSDAY
_____
_____
_____

FRIDAY
_____
_____
_____

SATURDAY
_____
_____
_____

SUNDAY
_____
_____
_____

THIS WEEK *Schedule*

MONDAY
AM | PM | AM | PM

TUESDAY
AM | PM | AM | PM

WEDNESDAY
AM | PM | AM | PM

THURSDAY
AM | PM | AM | PM

FRIDAY
AM | PM | AM | PM

SATURDAY
AM | PM | AM | PM

SUNDAY
AM | PM | AM | PM

THIS WEEK *Goals*

MONDAY _____
_____
_____

TUESDAY _____
_____
_____

WEDNESDAY _____
_____
_____

THURSDAY _____
_____
_____

FRIDAY _____
_____
_____

SATURDAY _____
_____
_____

SUNDAY _____
_____
_____

THIS WEEK *Schedule*

MONDAY
AM	PM	AM	PM

TUESDAY
AM	PM	AM	PM

WEDNESDAY
AM	PM	AM	PM

THURSDAY
AM	PM	AM	PM

FRIDAY
AM	PM	AM	PM

SATURDAY
AM	PM	AM	PM

SUNDAY
AM	PM	AM	PM

MID MONTH *Checklist*

Am I on track to accomplish my goals?

_____
_____
_____
_____
_____
_____

What are my accountability measures?

_____
_____
_____
_____
_____
_____

What have I accomplished so far?

_____
_____
_____
_____
_____
_____

On a scale from 1 to 10 how close am I toreaching my goals

○   ○   ○   ○   ○   ○   ○   ○   ○   ○
1   2   3   4   5   6   7   8   9   10

Notes

THIS WEEK *Goals*

MONDAY _____
_____
_____

TUESDAY _____
_____
_____

WEDNESDAY _____
_____
_____

THURSDAY _____
_____
_____

FRIDAY _____
_____
_____

SATURDAY _____
_____
_____

SUNDAY _____
_____
_____

THIS WEEK *Schedule*

MONDAY
AM	PM	AM	PM

TUESDAY
AM	PM	AM	PM

WEDNESDAY
AM	PM	AM	PM

THURSDAY
AM	PM	AM	PM

FRIDAY
AM	PM	AM	PM

SATURDAY
AM	PM	AM	PM

SUNDAY
AM	PM	AM	PM

THIS WEEK *Goals*

MONDAY _____
_____
_____

TUESDAY _____
_____
_____

WEDNESDAY _____
_____
_____

THURSDAY _____
_____
_____

FRIDAY _____
_____
_____

SATURDAY _____
_____
_____

SUNDAY _____
_____
_____

THIS WEEK *Schedule*

MONDAY
AM	PM	AM	PM

TUESDAY
AM	PM	AM	PM

WEDNESDAY
AM	PM	AM	PM

THURSDAY
AM	PM	AM	PM

FRIDAY
AM	PM	AM	PM

SATURDAY
AM	PM	AM	PM

SUNDAY
AM	PM	AM	PM

What did I accomplish this month?

_____
_____
_____
_____

Did I meet my goals?

_____
_____
_____
_____

If not, what do I need to do to differently to accomplish my goals?

_____
_____
_____
_____

A goal without a plan is
Just a Wish

THINK *Tank*

Think Tank n/-
A place where ideas are formed
Use this page to write about new ideas and things you are thinking about.

_____
_____
_____
_____
_____
_____
_____
_____
_____
_____
_____
_____
_____
_____
_____
_____
_____
_____
_____
_____
_____
_____
_____
_____

Affirmations

/afərˈmāSH(ə)n/
Words of encouragement and motivation.
Use this page to write motivational content.

_____
_____
_____
_____
_____
_____
_____
_____
_____
_____
_____
_____
_____
_____
_____
_____
_____
_____
_____
_____
_____
_____
_____
_____
_____
_____
_____

Notes

Month: _____

SUNDAY	MONDAY	TUESDAY	WEDNESDAY

THURSDAY	FRIDAY	SATURDAY

Notes

_____
_____
_____
_____
_____
_____
_____
_____
_____
_____
_____
_____
_____
_____
_____
_____
_____
_____
_____
_____
_____
_____
_____
_____
_____
_____
_____
_____
_____

THIS WEEK *Goals*

MONDAY _____
_____
_____

TUESDAY _____
_____
_____

WEDNESDAY _____
_____
_____

THURSDAY _____
_____
_____

FRIDAY _____
_____
_____

SATURDAY _____
_____
_____

SUNDAY _____
_____
_____

THIS WEEK *Schedule*

MONDAY
AM	PM	AM	PM

TUESDAY
AM	PM	AM	PM

WEDNESDAY
AM	PM	AM	PM

THURSDAY
AM	PM	AM	PM

FRIDAY
AM	PM	AM	PM

SATURDAY
AM	PM	AM	PM

SUNDAY
AM	PM	AM	PM

THIS WEEK *Goals*

MONDAY _____
_____
_____

TUESDAY _____
_____
_____

WEDNESDAY _____
_____
_____

THURSDAY _____
_____
_____

FRIDAY _____
_____
_____

SATURDAY _____
_____
_____

SUNDAY _____
_____
_____

THIS WEEK *Schedule*

MONDAY
AM | PM | AM | PM

TUESDAY
AM | PM | AM | PM

WEDNESDAY
AM | PM | AM | PM

THURSDAY
AM | PM | AM | PM

FRIDAY
AM | PM | AM | PM

SATURDAY
AM | PM | AM | PM

SUNDAY
AM | PM | AM | PM

MID MONTH *Checklist*

Am I on track to accomplish my goals?

_____
_____
_____
_____
_____
_____

What are my accountability measures?

_____
_____
_____
_____
_____
_____

What have I accomplished so far?

_____
_____
_____
_____
_____
_____

On a scale from 1 to 10 how close am I toreaching my goals

○   ○   ○   ○   ○   ○   ○   ○   ○   ○
1   2   3   4   5   6   7   8   9   10

Notes

THIS WEEK *Goals*

MONDAY
_____
_____
_____

TUESDAY
_____
_____
_____

WEDNESDAY
_____
_____
_____

THURSDAY
_____
_____
_____

FRIDAY
_____
_____
_____

SATURDAY
_____
_____
_____

SUNDAY
_____
_____
_____

THIS WEEK *Schedule*

MONDAY _____
AM	PM	AM	PM

TUESDAY _____
AM	PM	AM	PM

WEDNESDAY _____
AM	PM	AM	PM

THURSDAY _____
AM	PM	AM	PM

FRIDAY _____
AM	PM	AM	PM

SATURDAY _____
AM	PM	AM	PM

SUNDAY _____
AM	PM	AM	PM

THIS WEEK *Goals*

MONDAY
_____
_____
_____

TUESDAY
_____
_____
_____

WEDNESDAY
_____
_____
_____

THURSDAY
_____
_____
_____

FRIDAY
_____
_____
_____

SATURDAY
_____
_____
_____

SUNDAY
_____
_____
_____

THIS WEEK *Schedule*

MONDAY _____
AM   PM   AM   PM

TUESDAY _____
AM   PM   AM   PM

WEDNESDAY _____
AM   PM   AM   PM

THURSDAY _____
AM   PM   AM   PM

FRIDAY _____
AM   PM   AM   PM

SATURDAY _____
AM   PM   AM   PM

SUNDAY _____
AM   PM   AM   PM

MONTHLY *Closeout*

What did I accomplish this month?

_____
_____
_____
_____

Did I meet my goals?

_____
_____
_____
_____

If not, what do I need to do to differently to accomplish my goals?

_____
_____
_____
_____

A goal without a plan is
Just a Wish

THINK *Tank*

Think Tank n/-
A place where ideas are formed
Use this page to write about new ideas and things you are thinking about.

_____
_____
_____
_____
_____
_____
_____
_____
_____
_____
_____
_____
_____
_____
_____
_____
_____
_____
_____
_____
_____
_____
_____

Affirmations

/afərˈmāSH(ə)n/
Words of encouragement and motivation.
Use this page to write motivational content.

_____
_____
_____
_____
_____
_____
_____
_____
_____
_____
_____
_____
_____
_____
_____
_____
_____
_____
_____
_____
_____
_____
_____
_____
_____

Notes

Month: _____

SUNDAY	MONDAY	TUESDAY	WEDNESDAY

THURSDAY	FRIDAY	SATURDAY	Notes
			_____
			_____
			_____
			_____
			_____
			_____
			_____
			_____
			_____
			_____
			_____
			_____
			_____
			_____
			_____
			_____
			_____
			_____
			_____
			_____
			_____
			_____
			_____
			_____
			_____
			_____
			_____

THIS WEEK *Goals*

MONDAY _____

_____

_____

TUESDAY _____

_____

_____

WEDNESDAY _____

_____

_____

THURSDAY _____

_____

_____

FRIDAY _____

_____

_____

SATURDAY _____

_____

_____

SUNDAY _____

_____

_____

THIS WEEK *Schedule*

MONDAY
AM	PM	AM	PM

TUESDAY
AM	PM	AM	PM

WEDNESDAY
AM	PM	AM	PM

THURSDAY
AM	PM	AM	PM

FRIDAY
AM	PM	AM	PM

SATURDAY
AM	PM	AM	PM

SUNDAY
AM	PM	AM	PM

THIS WEEK *Goals*

MONDAY _____
_____
_____

TUESDAY _____
_____
_____

WEDNESDAY _____
_____
_____

THURSDAY _____
_____
_____

FRIDAY _____
_____
_____

SATURDAY _____
_____
_____

SUNDAY _____
_____
_____

THIS WEEK *Schedule*

MONDAY
AM   PM   AM   PM

TUESDAY
AM   PM   AM   PM

WEDNESDAY
AM   PM   AM   PM

THURSDAY
AM   PM   AM   PM

FRIDAY
AM   PM   AM   PM

SATURDAY
AM   PM   AM   PM

SUNDAY
AM   PM   AM   PM

MID MONTH *Checklist*

Am I on track to accomplish my goals?

_____
_____
_____
_____
_____
_____

What are my accountability measures?

_____
_____
_____
_____
_____
_____

What have I accomplished so far?

_____
_____
_____
_____
_____
_____

On a scale from 1 to 10 how close am I to reaching my goals

○   ○   ○   ○   ○   ○   ○   ○   ○   ○
1   2   3   4   5   6   7   8   9   10

Notes

THIS WEEK *Goals*

MONDAY _____
_____
_____

TUESDAY _____
_____
_____

WEDNESDAY _____
_____
_____

THURSDAY _____
_____
_____

FRIDAY _____
_____
_____

SATURDAY _____
_____
_____

SUNDAY _____
_____
_____

THIS WEEK *Schedule*

MONDAY

AM	PM	AM	PM

TUESDAY

AM	PM	AM	PM

WEDNESDAY

AM	PM	AM	PM

THURSDAY

AM	PM	AM	PM

FRIDAY

AM	PM	AM	PM

SATURDAY

AM	PM	AM	PM

SUNDAY

AM	PM	AM	PM

THIS WEEK *Goals*

MONDAY _____
_____
_____

TUESDAY _____
_____
_____

WEDNESDAY _____
_____
_____

THURSDAY _____
_____
_____

FRIDAY _____
_____
_____

SATURDAY _____
_____
_____

SUNDAY _____
_____
_____

THIS WEEK *Schedule*

MONDAY
AM | PM | AM | PM

TUESDAY
AM | PM | AM | PM

WEDNESDAY
AM | PM | AM | PM

THURSDAY
AM | PM | AM | PM

FRIDAY
AM | PM | AM | PM

SATURDAY
AM | PM | AM | PM

SUNDAY
AM | PM | AM | PM

MONTHLY *Closeout*

What did I accomplish this month?

_____
_____
_____
_____

Did I meet my goals?

_____
_____
_____
_____

If not, what do I need to do to differently to accomplish my goals?

_____
_____
_____
_____

A goal without a plan is
Just a Wish

THINK *Tank*

Think Tank n/-
A place where ideas are formed
Use this page to write about new ideas and things you are thinking about.

_____

_____

_____

_____

_____

_____

_____

_____

_____

_____

_____

_____

_____

_____

_____

_____

_____

_____

_____

_____

_____

_____

_____

Affirmations

/afərˈmāSH(ə)n/
Words of encouragement and motivation.
Use this page to write motivational content.

_____
_____
_____
_____
_____
_____
_____
_____
_____
_____
_____
_____
_____
_____
_____
_____
_____
_____
_____
_____
_____
_____
_____
_____
_____
_____

Don't let anything stop you from

Achieving Your

Goals

Month: _____

SUNDAY	MONDAY	TUESDAY	WEDNESDAY

THURSDAY	FRIDAY	SATURDAY

THIS WEEK *Goals*

MONDAY

_____
_____
_____

TUESDAY

_____
_____
_____

WEDNESDAY

_____
_____
_____

THURSDAY

_____
_____
_____

FRIDAY

_____
_____
_____

SATURDAY

_____
_____
_____

SUNDAY

_____
_____
_____

THIS WEEK *Schedule*

MONDAY
AM	PM	AM	PM

TUESDAY
AM	PM	AM	PM

WEDNESDAY
AM	PM	AM	PM

THURSDAY
AM	PM	AM	PM

FRIDAY
AM	PM	AM	PM

SATURDAY
AM	PM	AM	PM

SUNDAY
AM	PM	AM	PM

THIS WEEK *Goals*

MONDAY _____
_____
_____

TUESDAY _____
_____
_____

WEDNESDAY _____
_____
_____

THURSDAY _____
_____
_____

FRIDAY _____
_____
_____

SATURDAY _____
_____
_____

SUNDAY _____
_____
_____

THIS WEEK *Schedule*

MONDAY
AM | PM | AM | PM

TUESDAY
AM | PM | AM | PM

WEDNESDAY
AM | PM | AM | PM

THURSDAY
AM | PM | AM | PM

FRIDAY
AM | PM | AM | PM

SATURDAY
AM | PM | AM | PM

SUNDAY
AM | PM | AM | PM

MID MONTH *Checklist*

Am I on track to accomplish my goals?

_____
_____
_____
_____
_____
_____

What are my accountability measures?

_____
_____
_____
_____
_____
_____

What have I accomplished so far?

_____
_____
_____
_____
_____
_____

On a scale from 1 to 10 how close am I toreaching my goals

○ ○ ○ ○ ○ ○ ○ ○ ○ ○
1   2   3   4   5   6   7   8   9   10

Notes

THIS WEEK *Goals*

MONDAY _____
_____
_____

TUESDAY _____
_____
_____

WEDNESDAY _____
_____
_____

THURSDAY _____
_____
_____

FRIDAY _____
_____
_____

SATURDAY _____
_____
_____

SUNDAY _____
_____
_____

THIS WEEK *Schedule*

MONDAY

AM | PM | AM | PM

TUESDAY

AM | PM | AM | PM

WEDNESDAY

AM | PM | AM | PM

THURSDAY

AM | PM | AM | PM

FRIDAY

AM | PM | AM | PM

SATURDAY

AM | PM | AM | PM

SUNDAY

AM | PM | AM | PM

THIS WEEK *Goals*

MONDAY _____
_____
_____

TUESDAY _____
_____
_____

WEDNESDAY _____
_____
_____

THURSDAY _____
_____
_____

FRIDAY _____
_____
_____

SATURDAY _____
_____
_____

SUNDAY _____
_____
_____

THIS WEEK *Schedule*

MONDAY _____
AM	PM	AM	PM

TUESDAY _____
AM	PM	AM	PM

WEDNESDAY _____
AM	PM	AM	PM

THURSDAY _____
AM	PM	AM	PM

FRIDAY _____
AM	PM	AM	PM

SATURDAY _____
AM	PM	AM	PM

SUNDAY _____
AM	PM	AM	PM

What did I accomplish this month?

_____

_____

_____

_____

Did I meet my goals?

_____

_____

_____

_____

If not, what do I need to do to differently to accomplish my goals?

_____

_____

_____

_____

A goal without a plan is
Just a Wish

THINK *Tank*

Think Tank n/-
A place where ideas are formed
Use this page to write about new ideas and things you are thinking about.

_____
_____
_____
_____
_____
_____
_____
_____
_____
_____
_____
_____
_____
_____
_____
_____
_____
_____
_____
_____
_____

Affirmations

/əˈfərˈmāSH(ə)n/

Words of encouragement and motivation.
Use this page to write motivational content.

_____

_____

_____

_____

_____

_____

_____

_____

_____

_____

_____

_____

_____

_____

_____

_____

_____

_____

_____

_____

_____

_____

_____

_____

_____

_____

_____

_____

Notes

Month: _____

SUNDAY	MONDAY	TUESDAY	WEDNESDAY

THURSDAY	FRIDAY	SATURDAY	Notes

THIS WEEK *Goals*

MONDAY _____

_____

_____

TUESDAY _____

_____

_____

WEDNESDAY _____

_____

_____

THURSDAY _____

_____

_____

FRIDAY _____

_____

_____

SATURDAY _____

_____

_____

SUNDAY _____

_____

_____

THIS WEEK *Schedule*

MONDAY _____
AM · PM · AM · PM

TUESDAY _____
AM · PM · AM · PM

WEDNESDAY _____
AM · PM · AM · PM

THURSDAY _____
AM · PM · AM · PM

FRIDAY _____
AM · PM · AM · PM

SATURDAY _____
AM · PM · AM · PM

SUNDAY _____
AM · PM · AM · PM

THIS WEEK *Goals*

MONDAY _____
_____
_____

TUESDAY _____
_____
_____

WEDNESDAY _____
_____
_____

THURSDAY _____
_____
_____

FRIDAY _____
_____
_____

SATURDAY _____
_____
_____

SUNDAY _____
_____
_____

THIS WEEK *Schedule*

MONDAY
AM	PM	AM	PM

TUESDAY
AM	PM	AM	PM

WEDNESDAY
AM	PM	AM	PM

THURSDAY
AM	PM	AM	PM

FRIDAY
AM	PM	AM	PM

SATURDAY
AM	PM	AM	PM

SUNDAY
AM	PM	AM	PM

MID MONTH *Checklist*

Am I on track to accomplish my goals?

_____
_____
_____
_____
_____
_____

What are my accountability measures?

_____
_____
_____
_____
_____
_____

What have I accomplished so far?

_____
_____
_____
_____
_____
_____

On a scale from 1 to 10 how close am I to reaching my goals

○   ○   ○   ○   ○   ○   ○   ○   ○   ○
1   2   3   4   5   6   7   8   9   10

Notes

THIS WEEK *Goals*

MONDAY _____
_____
_____

TUESDAY _____
_____
_____

WEDNESDAY _____
_____
_____

THURSDAY _____
_____
_____

FRIDAY _____
_____
_____

SATURDAY _____
_____
_____

SUNDAY _____
_____
_____

THIS WEEK *Schedule*

MONDAY
AM	PM	AM	PM

TUESDAY
AM	PM	AM	PM

WEDNESDAY
AM	PM	AM	PM

THURSDAY
AM	PM	AM	PM

FRIDAY
AM	PM	AM	PM

SATURDAY
AM	PM	AM	PM

SUNDAY
AM	PM	AM	PM

THIS WEEK *Goals*

MONDAY _____
_____
_____

TUESDAY _____
_____
_____

WEDNESDAY _____
_____
_____

THURSDAY _____
_____
_____

FRIDAY _____
_____
_____

SATURDAY _____
_____
_____

SUNDAY _____
_____
_____

THIS WEEK *Schedule*

MONDAY _____

AM PM AM PM

TUESDAY _____

AM PM AM PM

WEDNESDAY _____

AM PM AM PM

THURSDAY _____

AM PM AM PM

FRIDAY _____

AM PM AM PM

SATURDAY _____

AM PM AM PM

SUNDAY _____

AM PM AM PM

What did I accomplish this month?

_____
_____
_____
_____

Did I meet my goals?

_____
_____
_____
_____

If not, what do I need to do to differently to accomplish my goals?

_____
_____
_____
_____

A goal without a plan is
Just a Wish

THINK *Tank*

Think Tank n/-
A place where ideas are formed
Use this page to write about new ideas and things you are thinking about.

_____
_____
_____
_____
_____
_____
_____
_____
_____
_____
_____
_____
_____
_____
_____
_____
_____
_____
_____
_____
_____

Affirmations

/afərˈmāSH(ə)n/
Words of encouragement and motivation.
Use this page to write motivational content.

_____
_____
_____
_____
_____
_____
_____
_____
_____
_____
_____
_____
_____
_____
_____
_____
_____
_____
_____
_____
_____
_____
_____
_____
_____

Notes

Month: _____

SUNDAY	MONDAY	TUESDAY	WEDNESDAY

THURSDAY	FRIDAY	SATURDAY

Notes

_____
_____
_____
_____
_____
_____
_____
_____
_____
_____
_____
_____
_____
_____
_____
_____
_____
_____
_____
_____
_____
_____
_____

THIS WEEK *Goals*

MONDAY

_____

TUESDAY

_____

WEDNESDAY

_____

THURSDAY

_____

FRIDAY

_____

SATURDAY

_____

SUNDAY

_____

THIS WEEK *Schedule*

MONDAY
AM · PM · AM · PM

TUESDAY
AM · PM · AM · PM

WEDNESDAY
AM · PM · AM · PM

THURSDAY
AM · PM · AM · PM

FRIDAY
AM · PM · AM · PM

SATURDAY
AM · PM · AM · PM

SUNDAY
AM · PM · AM · PM

THIS WEEK *Goals*

MONDAY _____
_____
_____

TUESDAY _____
_____
_____

WEDNESDAY _____
_____
_____

THURSDAY _____
_____
_____

FRIDAY _____
_____
_____

SATURDAY _____
_____
_____

SUNDAY _____
_____
_____

THIS WEEK *Schedule*

MONDAY
AM	PM	AM	PM

TUESDAY
AM	PM	AM	PM

WEDNESDAY
AM	PM	AM	PM

THURSDAY
AM	PM	AM	PM

FRIDAY
AM	PM	AM	PM

SATURDAY
AM	PM	AM	PM

SUNDAY
AM	PM	AM	PM

MID MONTH *Checklist*

Am I on track to accomplish my goals?

_____
_____
_____
_____
_____
_____

What are my accountability measures?

_____
_____
_____
_____
_____
_____

What have I accomplished so far?

_____
_____
_____
_____
_____
_____

On a scale from 1 to 10 how close am I toreaching my goals

○ ○ ○ ○ ○ ○ ○ ○ ○ ○
1   2   3   4   5   6   7   8   9   10

Notes

THIS WEEK *Goals*

MONDAY _____
_____
_____

TUESDAY _____
_____
_____

WEDNESDAY _____
_____
_____

THURSDAY _____
_____
_____

FRIDAY _____
_____
_____

SATURDAY _____
_____
_____

SUNDAY _____
_____
_____

THIS WEEK *Schedule*

MONDAY _____
AM   PM   AM   PM

TUESDAY _____
AM   PM   AM   PM

WEDNESDAY _____
AM   PM   AM   PM

THURSDAY _____
AM   PM   AM   PM

FRIDAY _____
AM   PM   AM   PM

SATURDAY _____
AM   PM   AM   PM

SUNDAY _____
AM   PM   AM   PM

THIS WEEK *Goals*

MONDAY _____
_____
_____

TUESDAY _____
_____
_____

WEDNESDAY _____
_____
_____

THURSDAY _____
_____
_____

FRIDAY _____
_____
_____

SATURDAY _____
_____
_____

SUNDAY _____
_____
_____

THIS WEEK *Schedule*

MONDAY
AM   PM   AM   PM

TUESDAY
AM   PM   AM   PM

WEDNESDAY
AM   PM   AM   PM

THURSDAY
AM   PM   AM   PM

FRIDAY
AM   PM   AM   PM

SATURDAY
AM   PM   AM   PM

SUNDAY
AM   PM   AM   PM

What did I accomplish this month?

_____
_____
_____
_____

Did I meet my goals?

_____
_____
_____
_____

If not, what do I need to do to differently to accomplish my goals?

_____
_____
_____
_____

A goal without a plan is
Just a Wish

THINK *Tank*

Think Tank n/-
A place where ideas are formed
Use this page to write about new ideas and things you are thinking about.

_____
_____
_____
_____
_____
_____
_____
_____
_____
_____
_____
_____
_____
_____
_____
_____
_____
_____
_____

Affirmations

/afərˈmāSH(ə)n/
Words of encouragement and motivation.
Use this page to write motivational content.

_____
_____
_____
_____
_____
_____
_____
_____
_____
_____
_____
_____
_____
_____
_____
_____
_____
_____
_____
_____
_____
_____
_____
_____
_____
_____

Notes

Month: _____

SUNDAY	MONDAY	TUESDAY	WEDNESDAY

THURSDAY	FRIDAY	SATURDAY	Notes
			_____
			_____
			_____
			_____
			_____
			_____
			_____
			_____
			_____
			_____
			_____
			_____
			_____
			_____
			_____
			_____
			_____
			_____
			_____
			_____
			_____
			_____
			_____
			_____
			_____
			_____

THIS WEEK *Goals*

MONDAY _____
_____
_____

TUESDAY _____
_____
_____

WEDNESDAY _____
_____
_____

THURSDAY _____
_____
_____

FRIDAY _____
_____
_____

SATURDAY _____
_____
_____

SUNDAY _____
_____
_____

THIS WEEK *Schedule*

MONDAY
AM	PM	AM	PM

TUESDAY
AM	PM	AM	PM

WEDNESDAY
AM	PM	AM	PM

THURSDAY
AM	PM	AM	PM

FRIDAY
AM	PM	AM	PM

SATURDAY
AM	PM	AM	PM

SUNDAY
AM	PM	AM	PM

THIS WEEK *Goals*

MONDAY _____
_____
_____

TUESDAY _____
_____
_____

WEDNESDAY _____
_____
_____

THURSDAY _____
_____
_____

FRIDAY _____
_____
_____

SATURDAY _____
_____
_____

SUNDAY _____
_____
_____

THIS WEEK *Schedule*

MONDAY
AM | PM | AM | PM

TUESDAY
AM | PM | AM | PM

WEDNESDAY
AM | PM | AM | PM

THURSDAY
AM | PM | AM | PM

FRIDAY
AM | PM | AM | PM

SATURDAY
AM | PM | AM | PM

SUNDAY
AM | PM | AM | PM

MID MONTH *Checklist*

Am I on track to accomplish my goals?

_____
_____
_____
_____
_____
_____

What are my accountability measures?

_____
_____
_____
_____
_____
_____

What have I accomplished so far?

_____
_____
_____
_____
_____
_____

On a scale from 1 to 10 how close am I toreaching my goals

○ ○ ○ ○ ○ ○ ○ ○ ○ ○
1 2 3 4 5 6 7 8 9 10

Notes

THIS WEEK *Goals*

MONDAY _____

_____

_____

TUESDAY _____

_____

_____

WEDNESDAY _____

_____

_____

THURSDAY _____

_____

_____

FRIDAY _____

_____

_____

SATURDAY _____

_____

_____

SUNDAY _____

_____

_____

THIS WEEK *Schedule*

MONDAY
AM	PM	AM	PM

TUESDAY
AM	PM	AM	PM

WEDNESDAY
AM	PM	AM	PM

THURSDAY
AM	PM	AM	PM

FRIDAY
AM	PM	AM	PM

SATURDAY
AM	PM	AM	PM

SUNDAY
AM	PM	AM	PM

THIS WEEK *Goals*

MONDAY
_____
_____
_____

TUESDAY
_____
_____
_____

WEDNESDAY
_____
_____
_____

THURSDAY
_____
_____
_____

FRIDAY
_____
_____
_____

SATURDAY
_____
_____
_____

SUNDAY
_____
_____
_____

THIS WEEK *Schedule*

MONDAY
AM	PM	AM	PM

TUESDAY
AM	PM	AM	PM

WEDNESDAY
AM	PM	AM	PM

THURSDAY
AM	PM	AM	PM

FRIDAY
AM	PM	AM	PM

SATURDAY
AM	PM	AM	PM

SUNDAY
AM	PM	AM	PM

What did I accomplish this month?

_____

_____

_____

_____

Did I meet my goals?

_____

_____

_____

_____

If not, what do I need to do to differently to accomplish my goals?

_____

_____

_____

_____

A goal without a plan is
Just a Wish

THINK *Tank*

Think Tank n/-
A place where ideas are formed
Use this page to write about new ideas and things you are thinking about.

_____
_____
_____
_____
_____
_____
_____
_____
_____
_____
_____
_____
_____
_____
_____
_____
_____
_____
_____
_____
_____
_____
_____

Affirmations

/afərˈmāSH(ə)n/
Words of encouragement and motivation.
Use this page to write motivational content.

_____
_____
_____
_____
_____
_____
_____
_____
_____
_____
_____
_____
_____
_____
_____
_____
_____
_____
_____
_____
_____
_____
_____
_____
_____
_____
_____

If it doesn't
Challenge You
it won't
Change You

www.ingramcontent.com/pod-product-compliance
Lightning Source LLC
Chambersburg PA
CBHW051850210326
41597CB00033B/5843